SEASONAL WEATHER

SPRING WEATHER

John Mason

The Bookwright Press
New York • 1991

Seasonal Weather

Spring Weather   Autumn Weather
Summer Weather   Winter Weather

Cover: Cherry blossom in a Japanese garden in spring.
Opposite: Dark rain clouds gather in the distance, as a rainbow forms over a field of ripening grain in spring.

First published in 1990 by
Wayland (Publishers) Ltd
61 Western Road, Hove
East Sussex, BN3 1JD, England

First published in the
United States in 1991 by
The Bookwright Press
387 Park Avenue South
New York, NY 10016

Library of Congress Cataloging-in-Publication Data
Mason, John.
    Spring weather / by John Mason.
        p. cm. — (Seasonal weather)
    "First published in 1990 by Wayland (Publishers) Ltd. . . . Hove,
East Sussex . . . England"—T.p. verso.
    Includes bibliographical references and index.
    Summary: Explores all of the climatic changes that signify the spring
season around the world.
    ISBN 0-531-18437-4
    1. Spring—Juvenile literature. 2. Weather—Juvenile literature.
3. Rain and rainfall—Measurement—Juvenile literature. [1. Spring.
2. Weather. 3. Climatic changes, 4. Rain and rainfall.] I. Title.
II. Series: Mason, John. Seasonal weather.
QB637.5.M37 1991   90—14397
551.6—dc20   CIP
                                  AC

Typeset by Nicola Taylor, Wayland
Printed by Casterman S.A., Belgium

CONTENTS

What is spring?

In parts of the world there are clear changes in the weather during the year. These changes are called seasons. There are four seasons – spring, summer, autumn and winter. Each season has a particular type of weather and is marked by differences in the length of day and night. The long days have plenty of sunshine, and it is warmer than when days are short.

In the **tropics** it is always warm. Day and night are of roughly equal length all year.

Close to the **Equator** it is very hot with heavy rain through-out the year. Elsewhere in the tropics there is a hot, wet season and a cooler, dry season. Near the **poles** it is always bitterly cold. There are only two real seasons, summer and winter, but the **Arctic** has a short spring and autumn with warmer temperatures. Only in the mild **temperate regions**, which lie between the polar regions and the tropics, are changes between all four seasons very marked.

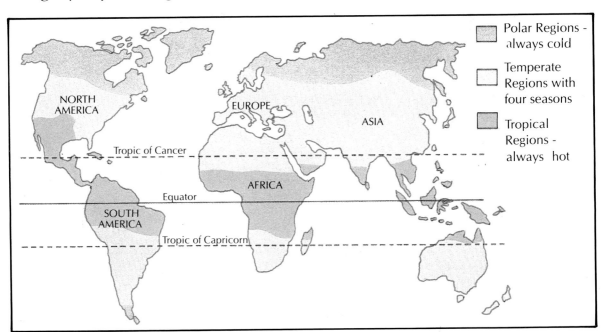

A map of the world showing the main regions of climate.

Colorful alpine flowers carpet the mountain slopes in the spring.

Spring occurs as winter changes to summer. Short, cold winter days gradually become longer and warmer. The Sun rises higher in the sky and sets later each evening. As the hours of daylight grow longer and the nights shorter and warmer, we feel the approach of summer.

The Earth and the seasons

Every year the Earth moves around the Sun. The Earth spins on its **axis**, which leans over at an angle of 23.5°. This tilt means that as the Earth travels around the Sun, first the northern **hemisphere** then the southern hemisphere is tilted toward the Sun.

Northern Hemisphere			
Autumn	Winter	Spring	Summer
September	December	March	June
October	January	April	July
November	February	May	August
Spring	Summer	Autumn	Winter
Southern Hemisphere			

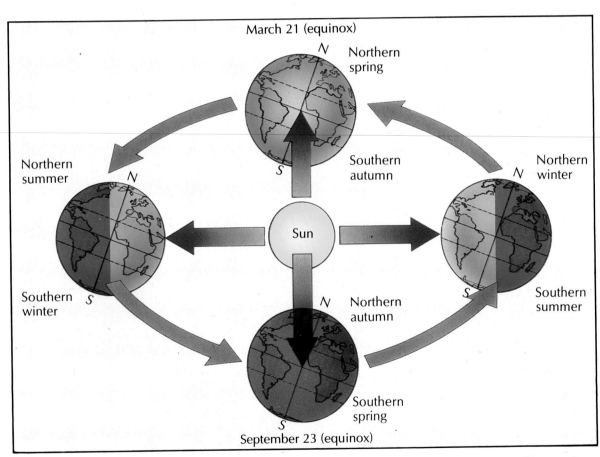

As the Earth travels around the Sun each year, the tilt of its axis affects the amount of sunlight and heat that reaches different parts of the Earth through the year. This gives us the changing seasons.

Each hemisphere in turn receives more sunlight and heat than the other. The amount of heat received at any place varies through the year. This causes the seasons.

Between March 21 and September 23, the northern hemisphere is tilted toward the Sun. This means that in temperate regions the days are long, the nights are short, and the weather is warm. At the same time in the southern hemisphere, the Sun remains lower in the sky, the days are short, and the weather is cold. Between September 23 and March 21, the reverse is true, and it is cold in the northern hemisphere and warm in the south.

Since the seasons are reversed in the two hemispheres, when it is spring in one hemisphere it is autumn in the other. The northern spring begins about March 21. In the southern hemisphere, that is about the start of autumn. Southern spring begins about September 23, the beginning of the northern autumn. Both these dates mark the time of year when day and night are of equal length all over the world. They are called equinoxes.

It is October and jacaranda trees are blossoming in the Botanical Gardens in Sydney, Australia, in the spring. At the same time in the northern hemisphere, leaves are falling from the trees and it is autumn.

The spring season

Spring weather can be very unsettled. Many days are warm and sunny, but it can get cold at night. In early spring there can be heavy frosts and fog on cold nights. Spring is cooler than autumn because it takes time for the spring sunshine to melt snow and ice from the cold winter season. Only then can the Sun begin to warm the land, sea and air. With the increasing warmth, plants begin to grow, new crops are planted, and flowers start to bloom in gardens and in the countryside.

Spring occurs early in the temperate regions near the tropics. Here the weather is always warmer. By mid-April, for example, southern California and the Mediterranean countries can be as warm as Britain or Belgium in midsummer. In temperate lands near the polar regions, spring arrives later.

As spring sunshine melts snow and ice that have built up during the winter, there may be flooding. In the mountains, sunshine, warm rain and wind may loosen huge masses of snow on

Early spring is a busy time for farmers. When the frost and snow have melted, farmers plow their fields ready for planting crops.

◄ Low cloud and mist linger on a rainy spring day over the mountains in County Down, Northern Ireland.

▼ An avalanche crashes down a mountain slope in the French Alps.

mountain slopes. These **avalanches** crash down on valleys below and can be very destructive. In the European Alps, whole villages have been swept away or buried by avalanches.

Fastest Avalanches

One of the fastest avalanches occurred at Glarnisch in Switzerland on March 6, 1898.

Snow traveled down a 44° slope at an average speed of 217 mph (349 kph) covering a distance of 4.3 mi (6.9 km) in 72 seconds.

The Earth's atmosphere

Seen from space, the Earth is partly hidden by clouds. Clouds occur only in the layer of the **atmosphere** nearest the ground. Nine-tenths of the Earth's air is contained in this shallow layer, called the troposphere. It extends to a height of about 5 mi (8 km) at the poles and 10 mi (16 km) at the Equator.

All the Earth's weather systems occur in the troposphere. It consists mainly of the gases nitrogen and oxygen, with a little carbon dioxide and water vapor. The water vapor produces the clouds that give us rain, hail and snow.

Above the troposphere, the air gets thinner. A layer called the stratosphere reaches a height of about 30 mi (50 km). It contains a small amount of . the gas **ozone**, which as we shall see later is very important. Above the strato-sphere lies another layer, the mesosphere. Beyond this, the ionosphere extends into space.

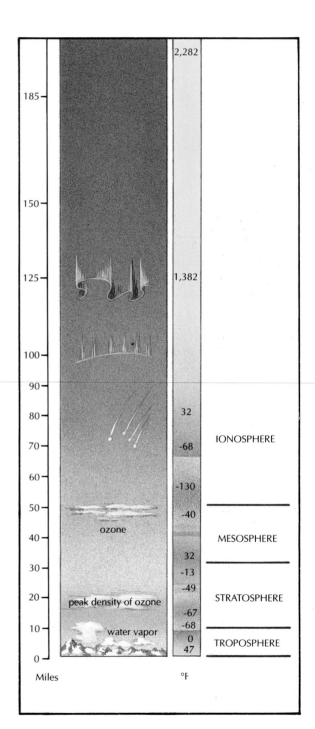

The main zones and temperatures up through the atmosphere.

▲ **The Moon rising above the upper layers of the Earth's atmosphere.**

The air in the atmosphere pushes down on the Earth's surface causing **air pressure**. Because the air gets thinner, air pressure gets less as one travels upward. Air pressure also varies from one place to another on the Earth's surface. Differences in air pressure in different parts of the world create the Earth's winds.

◀ **As the hot-air balloon rises, the air pressure around it lessens.**

The wind

The Earth's winds are created by differences in air pressure. The Sun heats the Earth unevenly, causing air in some places to be warmer than air in other parts. Warm air expands and becomes lighter. It rises, creating an area of low pressure beneath it. Cool air is heavier and it sinks, forming a region of high pressure. Air will always try to move from high pressure toward low pressure, causing winds to blow.

Strong winds that usually blow from the same direction are called prevailing winds. Trade winds, westerlies and polar easterlies are the Earth's main prevailing winds. However, sometimes there are variations in the wind patterns. These occur near oceans and lakes or within local regions of high- or low-pressure air. This may cause local winds to blow.

Strong local winds often blow in spring. Cold, northerly winds called the mistral are common in southern France. They become stronger as they blow down the Rhône valley.

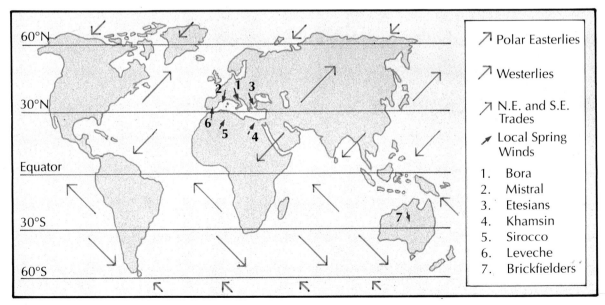

The world's major winds and some local winds that blow in the spring.

Similar winds occur in the northern Adriatic (the bora) and Aegean Seas (the etesians) when cold northerly winds are forced up over the mountains.

Warm, dry southerly winds blow across North Africa in late spring, becoming moist if they travel over the sea. These are called the sirocco in Algeria, the leveche in southeast Spain, and the khamsin in Egypt and the eastern Mediterranean. Hot, dry northerly winds called "brickfielders" blow over central Australia.

▲ A strong northerly wind, the mistral, sometimes blows down the beautiful Rhône Valley, France, in the spring.

◄ A tree on Norfolk Island, lying east of Australia, that has been bent by the prevailing wind.

Clouds and the water cycle

As the Sun warms the oceans, some water **evaporates** and turns into water vapor. Wherever air is warmed over sea or land, it absorbs water vapor, because warm air can hold more water vapor than cold air. As the warm air rises it cools and becomes less able to hold so much water vapor. At the **dewpoint** temperature, some of the water vapor **condenses** into small water droplets. These collect together to become visible as clouds.

If a cloud is blown into a patch of warmer air, some of the droplets turn back into water vapor and the cloud gets smaller. If the cloud is cooled, more water vapor condenses and the cloud grows. Cooled further still, the water droplets grow so large that they fall to the ground as rain, hail or snow.

Over land, rain sinks into the soil and is taken in by plants. Some of this moisture is given off by the plants' leaves and returned to the air.

Dark rain clouds bring showers during unsettled days in the spring.

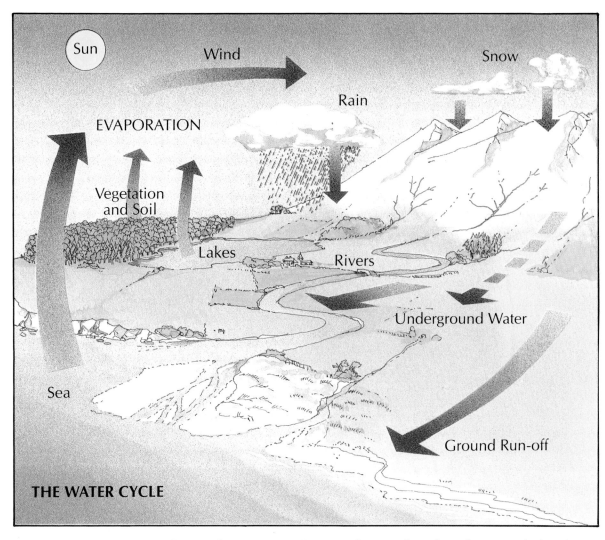

THE WATER CYCLE

The sea loses water through evaporation to form clouds. The precipitation from clouds often falls over land and runs back down to the sea.

Some water sinks deep into the soil and rocks below. Some rocks allow this ground water to seep through. It returns to the surface as springs, the sources of rivers.

Surface water flows directly into rivers and streams. All the water eventually reaches the sea and the process is repeated. This continual movement of water is called the water cycle.

Weather systems and fronts

An area of high-pressure air is called an anticyclone. In an anticyclone, cool air is slowly sinking. As it does so, it warms and dries out. In late spring, high pressure usually brings warm, dry weather. In a low-pressure region, or depression, warm air is rising, cooling and becoming wetter. This leads to the formation of clouds and rain. Depressions usually bring wet or stormy weather. As the winds blow, they cause the regions of high pressure and low pressure to move.

Cold and warm air do not mix. When they meet along a line called a **front**, the heavier cool air forces itself under the warm air, pushing it upward. Clouds form along the front,

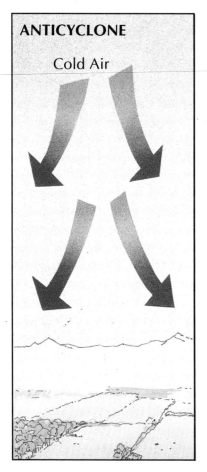

ANTICYCLONE

Cold Air

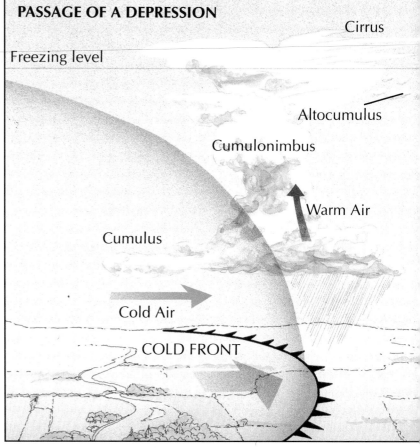

PASSAGE OF A DEPRESSION

Cirrus

Freezing level

Altocumulus

Cumulonimbus

Warm Air

Cumulus

Cold Air

COLD FRONT

bringing rain. Fronts may travel quite fast, and rain showers can be quickly followed by bright sunshine. Such changeable weather is common in the spring over northern Europe, where fronts sweep in overland from the Atlantic Ocean.

More settled weather occurs in other parts of the world, particularly near the tropics. In the center of large continental land masses in the late spring, the Sun's heat causes the air above the ground to rise, and depressions form. Some of these regions have heavy rain in the late afternoon as warm, moist air rises and cools, forming clouds that may bring heavy showers.

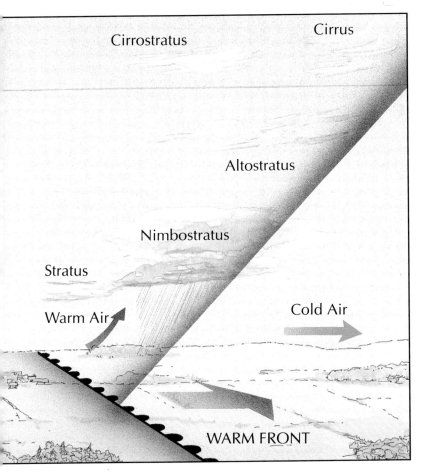

Cirrus
Cirrostratus
Altostratus
Nimbostratus
Stratus
Warm Air
Cold Air
WARM FRONT

(Far left) In an anticyclone, cold air is sinking. As it does so it warms and dries out.

(Left) Two fronts are formed around a depression: a warm front ahead and a cold front behind. At the warm front, the warm air rises over cold air, condenses, and heavy clouds and rain form. At a cold front, the heavier cold air wedges under warm air ahead of it. As the warm air is pushed upward, clouds and rain occur.

Spring in temperate lands

In northern Europe, the weather is quite changeable from early April until June. However, spring is the driest season of the year in the British Isles, northern France, northern Germany and Scandinavia, although it can be cool and cloudy. Cool temperatures are usual in early May, but later in May and early June, warm, dry settled weather is more common.

In Mediterranean countries, the long, unsettled spring lasts from March to May, with many false starts of summer

▲ A fine spring day in the Mediterranean harbor town of Liguria, in Italy.

Picking tulips in the colorful bulb fields of the Netherlands.

weather. April is usually a dry month in the eastern Mediterranean. Cyprus normally has only three days with 0.04 in (1 mm) of rainfall or more, but can get heavy rain when depressions move northeastward from north Africa. In March 1966, a depression moving across the eastern Mediterranean brought 2.8 in (70 mm) of rain to the Hanegev Desert in Israel in just four hours.

Near the polar regions, spring comes late. In northern parts of Canada and the USSR, snow may not start to thaw until late May, but most has gone by late June or early July. By late July, sea ice near the Arctic is breaking up. Snowstorms and heavy frosts may occur as late as mid-June.

Sea ice breaking up in the spring sunshine in Hudson Bay, Canada.

Spring around the world

In some parts of the world, the change from winter to summer is sudden, with hardly any spring in between. This occurs in the center of large continental land masses. In only a week or two, snow on the ground melts and temperatures soar toward summer levels. In the Mississippi Valley and the Great Plains of North America, warm southerly winds sweep up from the Gulf of Mexico. They not only melt the snow but create fierce whirlwinds called tornadoes, which hurl trees and houses into the air and overturn cars.

Between March and May in southern Asia, the Sun moves northward, heating the land and the air above it. This warm air rises, creating a marked area of low pressure. In early June, southeast trade

Flowers growing in the Kalahari Desert, Africa, after heavy rain.

winds are sucked across the Equator into this low-pressure region, becoming southwest winds. These **monsoon** winds are warm and moist, and when they reach land, they produce heavy rain.

In the dry desert regions of the world, springlike weather happens only when there is a very rare fall of rain. It is not a true season, but flowers and other plants suddenly appear immediately after the first rains, as though it were the spring season.

▲ Planting rice seedlings in the paddy fields of southern Thailand before the monsoon rains arrive.

Spring Tornadoes

In the spring of 1977 violent tornadoes occurred in the Madaripur district of Bangladesh, 81 mi (130 km) from Dacca.

Over 500 people were killed, more than 6,000 injured and hundreds of thousands made homeless.

The dark funnel of a spring tornado touches down 30 mi (50 km) east of Phoenix, Arizona.

Rainbows and haloes

A rainbow may be seen if the Sun is fairly low in the sky and breaks through the clouds, shining brightly, while rain is falling. A raindrop can "break up" sunlight into the colors of the **spectrum**, just as a glass prism does. You have to stand with the Sun behind you and be looking toward the falling raindrops to be able to see a rainbow clearly.

Different colors of light are bent or refracted by different amounts as they pass through raindrops. They are reflected off the backs of the drops at different angles. If one reflection occurs inside each drop, a primary rainbow forms. This has the strongest colors. The outer edge of the bow is red and the inner edge is violet.

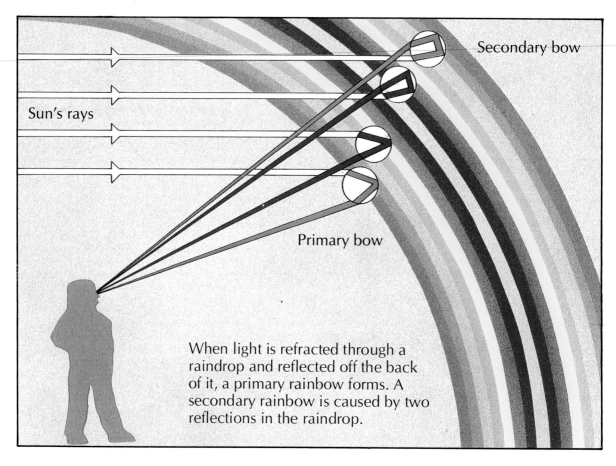

Sun's rays

Secondary bow

Primary bow

When light is refracted through a raindrop and reflected off the back of it, a primary rainbow forms. A secondary rainbow is caused by two reflections in the raindrop.

◄ A primary rainbow, with a fainter, secondary rainbow above it set against dark shower clouds in the spring.

▼ Mock suns, or sun-dogs, are images of the Sun formed by the refraction of light through ice crystals.

A secondary rainbow, caused by two reflections, sometimes appears above the primary bow. Its colors are reversed, the outer edge being violet and the inner one red. Its colors are fainter because light is lost at every reflection.

When the Moon shines through thin cloud, it may be surrounded by colored rings. This effect is called a corona. Water droplets split the light into colored bands. If the Sun or Moon shines through a thin layer of ice crystals, such as **cirrostratus** cloud, a faint colored halo may be seen around it.

The ozone hole

Sunlight contains more than just the light we can see. Invisible **ultraviolet** rays give sunbathers their summer tan, but over-exposure can cause skin cancer and eye cataracts. Too much ultraviolet also damages plants and life in the sea. Fortunately a thin layer in the stratosphere prevents 90 percent of the harmful ultraviolet rays from reaching the ground. This is the ozone layer, from 12 to 22 mi (20 to 35 km) above the ground.

A hole in the ozone layer over **Antarctica** was first noticed in October 1982. Nearly all the ozone there is destroyed in the first few weeks of spring. The cause appears to be artificially-made chemicals called **CFCs**. These are used in aerosol cans, fast-food packaging, air-conditioning and refrigerators.

In the darkness of the Antarctic winter, the air is very cold and no wind blows. In these conditions the CFCs

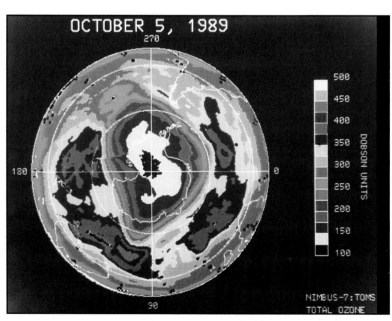

A satellite image of the ozone hole over the South Pole. The hole is the white area with the central black region.

The Ozone Hole

A group of scientific experts found that between 1969 and 1986 there were decreases in ozone from 1.7 to 3 percent over Europe, the U. S. and Japan and much of the USSR, China and the Middle East.

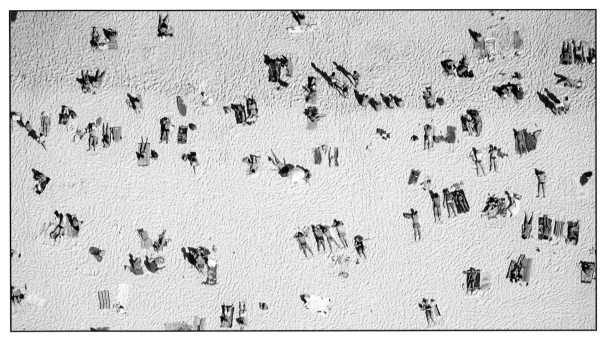

Sunbathers lying out on this beach in Australia are at risk from over-exposure to dangerous ultraviolet rays.

build up. The return of the Sun encourages the CFCs to attack the ozone layer. Later, the wind returns to mix the air. The ozone hole "repairs" itself, but it never totally disappears.

In October 1987, and again in 1989, the Antarctic ozone hole covered an area about the size of the United States. The outcome will be very serious if swift action is not taken to protect the Earth's ozone layer.

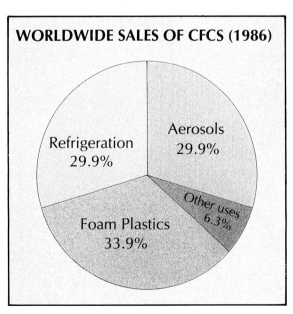

WORLDWIDE SALES OF CFCS (1986)

Refrigeration 29.9%

Aerosols 29.9%

Other uses 6.3%

Foam Plastics 33.9%

CFCs are used all over the world in a variety of products.

Weather forecasting

Information on the weather is collected from weather satellites, balloons, ships, aircraft and local weather stations around the world, and it is fed into large computers. These calculate the weather conditions at thousands of places on the Earth. The results are drawn on maps to help forecast the weather in the days ahead.

Weather maps show the roughly circular pressure areas, marked "high" for anticyclones and "low" for depressions. The lines around the pressure centers are called **isobars**. Winds tend to blow along the isobars. Isobars that are close together indicate strong winds.

Depressions cause unsettled weather in the spring in the temperate regions. Anticyclones usually bring settled weather. In late spring, they may bring a period of warm, sunny days, but earlier in the season they can bring cooler weather and fog.

Fronts are shown on weather maps as lines with triangles (cold fronts) or semicircles (warm fronts) drawn on them. An occluded front occurs when a warm front, which is slow-moving, is overtaken by a faster-moving cold front.

The weather map (opposite) shows a high over parts of the United States in the spring. A high over this Texas prairie is causing very fine spring weather.

An occluded front is drawn on a weather map as a line with triangles on one side and semicircles on the other.

Warm fronts move more slowly than cold fronts because the air is heavier and more difficult for the wind to push.

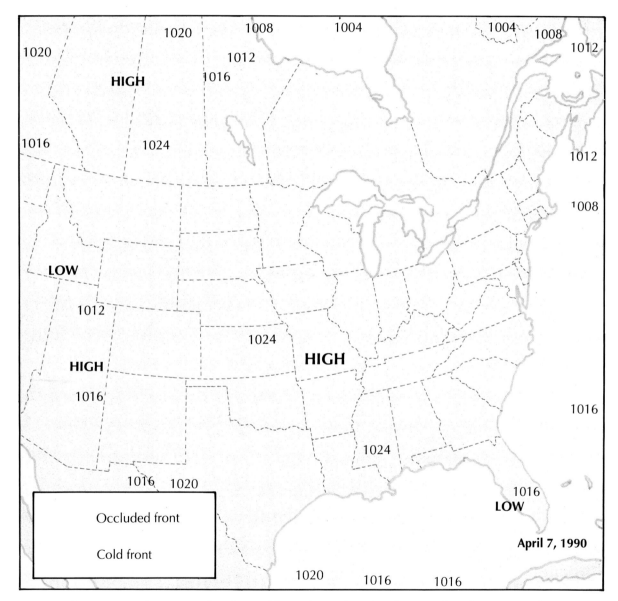

A weather map for a typical April spring day in the United States, showing high- and low-pressure centers and several fronts.

Things to do – measuring rainfall

To measure the amount of rainfall, you must make a rain gauge.

You will need:

- **A straight-sided glass jar, with a flat bottom, 5 in (125 mm) in diameter.**
- **A funnel with a top 5 in (125 mm) across, that will fit into the neck of the glass jar.**
- **A strip of white paper cut to the height of the jar, marked in inches by using a ruler.**
- **Waterproof tape.**
- **Modeling clay.**

Stick the paper scale on the outside of the jar using the waterproof tape. Make sure that the scale faces inward so you can read it by looking through the glass. Check to see that the bottom of the scale is exactly level with the bottom of the jar, allowing for the thickness of the glass.

Place the funnel in the top of the jar. Make sure it is fixed firmly, and that it is watertight by putting a layer of modeling clay between the jar and the funnel.

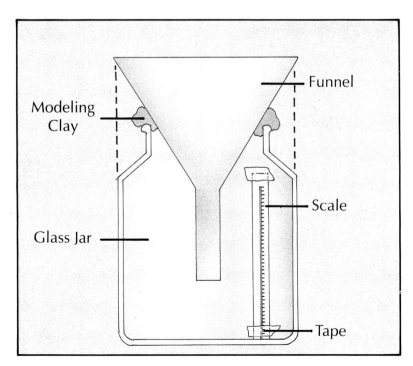

Modeling Clay

Glass Jar

Funnel

Scale

Tape

A diagram showing how the rain gauge is assembled and made ready for use.

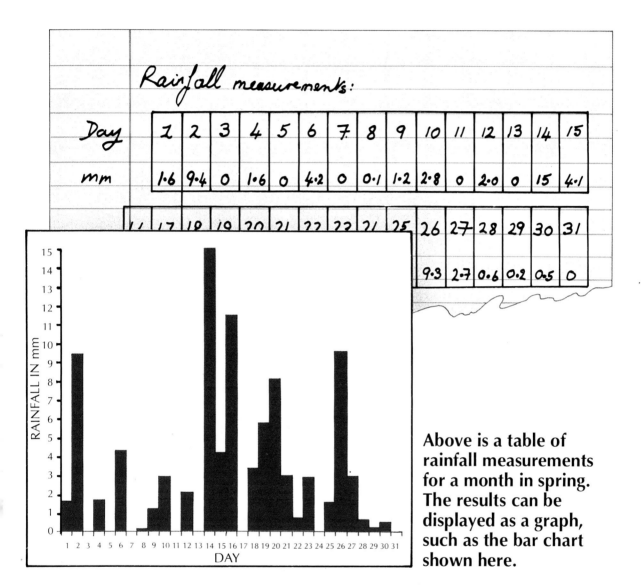

Rainfall measurements:

Day	1	2	3	4	5	6	7	8	9	10	11	12	13	14	15
mm	1.6	9.4	0	1.6	0	4.2	0	0.1	1.2	2.8	0	2.0	0	15	4.1

Day	16	17	18	19	20	21	22	23	24	25	26	27	28	29	30	31
mm											9.3	2.7	0.6	0.2	0.5	0

Above is a table of rainfall measurements for a month in spring. The results can be displayed as a graph, such as the bar chart shown here.

Position your rain gauge outside on an open area of ground away from buildings and trees. Record the depth of rainwater in it each day at the same time, then empty it and dry it carefully.

By recording your daily measurements in a notebook, you can total up the rainfall for each month. At the end of the year, you can draw a graph of weekly or monthly rainfall totals.

GLOSSARY

Air pressure A force exerted by layers of air on those below and on the ground.

Antarctica The very cold land mass at the South Pole.

Arctic The cold lands and seas around the North Pole.

Atmosphere The thin layer of gases surrounding the Earth.

Avalanche A mass of snow and ice that slides rapidly down the slopes of a mountain.

Axis An imaginary line about which the Earth spins once every day.

CFCs Artificially-made chemicals called chlorofluorocarbons that can damage the ozone layer.

Cirrostratus Thin milky-colored clouds that often produce rain.

Condense To turn from water vapor into drops of liquid as a result of cooling.

Dewpoint The temperature at which water vapor condenses, or turns into drops of liquid.

Equator An imaginary line encircling the Earth midway between the North and South Poles.

Evaporate To change into a vapor, as when liquid water becomes a vapor or gas due to heating.

Front The boundary between regions of warm and cooler air.

Hemisphere Half of the globe, divided into north and south.

Isobar A line on a weather map joining places with the same air pressure.

Monsoon A wind that changes direction with the seasons.

Ozone A gas found in the stratosphere. Ozone filters out harmful ultraviolet rays from sunlight.

Poles The extreme north and south points on the Earth.

Spectrum The colors produced (red, orange, yellow, green, blue, indigo, violet) when white sunlight is split into the colors that make it up.

Temperate regions The areas between the tropics and the poles that have a moderate, mild climate.

Tropics The areas each side of the Equator that are always warm.

Ultraviolet Invisible rays of light beyond violet in the visible spectrum.

BOOKS TO READ

Spring by Louis Santrey (Troll Assoc., 1982)
Spring Festivals by Mike Rosen (Bookwright, 1991)
Weather by Martin Bramwell (Watts, 1988)
Weather by Pierre Kohler (Barron, 1988)
Young Scientists Explore the Weather by Jerry De Bruin (Good Apple, 1983)

PICTURE ACKNOWLEDGMENTS

The publishers would like to thank the following for allowing their photographs to be reproduced in this book: Bruce Coleman Ltd 5 (Hans Reinhard), 19 (Bob and Clara Calhoun), 21 (top) (C.B Frith), 26 (John Shaw); Eye Ubiquitous *cover*; J.Allen Cash Ltd 9 (top), 13 (both), 14; Oxford Scientific Films 20, 23 (bottom); Photri 11 (top); Science Photo Library 24; Tony Stone Worldwide *inside cover*, 7, 8, 9 (bottom), 18 (both), 23 (top), 25; Topham 21 (bottom); Zefa 11 (bottom). All illustrations by Malcolm S. Walker except for page 6 by the Hayward Art Group.

INDEX

Numbers in **bold** refer to illustrations